WHAT DO YOU KNOW ABOUT

DIVORCE
and separation

PETE SANDERS and STEVE MYERS

COPPER BEECH BOOKS
BROOKFIELD, CONNECTICUT

Designed and produced by
Aladdin Books Ltd
28 Percy Street
London W1P 0LD

First published
in the United States in 1997 by
Copper Beech Books,
an imprint of The Millbrook Press
2 Old New Milford Road
Brookfield, Connecticut 06804

Printed in Belgium

Design   David West
                  Children's
                  Book Design
Editor   Sarah Levete
Illustrator   Mike Lacey
Picture Research Brooks Krikler
                  Research

Library of Congress Cataloging-in-Publication Data

Sanders, Pete.
Divorce and separation / Pete Sanders
and Steve Myers.
    p. cm. — (What do you know about)
Includes index.
Summary: Discusses the meaning of
separation and divorce and some of the
reasons that relationships come to an end.
Also examines the effects that divorce and
separation can have on people's lives.
ISBN 0-7613-0574-2
1. Divorce—Juvenile literature.
2. Separation (Psychology)—Juvenile
literature. 3. Children of divorced
parents—Attitudes—Juvenile literature.
[1. Divorce. 2. Separation (Psychology)]
I. Myers, Steve. II. Titles. III. Series:
Sanders, Pete. What do you know about.
HQ814.S26 1997   96-35822
306.89—dc20   CIP AC

CONTENTS

HOW TO USE THIS BOOK
The books in this series are intended to help young people to understand more about issues that may affect their lives.

Each book can be read by a child alone, or together with a parent, teacher, or helper. Issues raised in the storyline are further discussed in the accompanying text, so that there is an opportunity to talk through ideas as they come up.

At the end of the book there is a section called "What Can We Do?" This gives practical ideas which will be useful for both young people and adults. Organizations and helplines are also listed, to provide the reader with additional sources of information and support.

INTRODUCTION

TODAY, DIVORCE AND SEPARATION ARE WIDELY CONSIDERED AS ACCEPTABLE CHOICES FOR PEOPLE WHO ARE NO LONGER HAPPY IN THEIR RELATIONSHIP.

An increasing number of young people may, at some point in their lives, have to deal with the divorce or separation of parents or other close relatives.

This book explains what divorce and separation mean, and looks at some of the reasons that relationships come to an end. It considers the effects that divorce and separation can have on people's lives. Each chapter introduces a different aspect of the subject, illustrated by a continuing storyline. The characters in the story face situations and feelings which many people will experience. After each episode, we look at some of the issues raised, and broaden the discussion. By the end, you will understand more about how divorce and separation can affect families, and the emotions which might have to be faced.

RELATIONSHIPS

FOR MANY PEOPLE, RELATIONSHIPS MAKE A HUGE DIFFERENCE IN THE QUALITY OF THEIR LIVES. SHARING EXPERIENCES WITH OTHER PEOPLE CAN ADD TO OUR OWN ENJOYMENT OF THEM.

At some point in their lives, many adults will form an intimate and long-lasting relationship with another person.
Couples might declare their commitment to each other by deciding to marry. Or they may live together without being married. The decision will depend on the people involved and their own attitudes and beliefs. For most people, getting to know someone very well before beginning this kind of partnership is of great importance. How a relationship begins can affect the way it develops. Rushing into things can present possible problems later on. People's attitudes, values, and interests often change as time goes by, and this can put a strain on even very close relationships. Although there are ups and downs in any relationship, it is important to remember that sometimes they do end, even though we might not want them to.

Throughout our lives, we are involved in relationships with other people. Some may be casual acquaintances, while others become good friends. Within any family, there are many different types of relationships. Good relationships and friendships can add to our own sense of well-being and happiness.

▽ One day after school, Ruben Sharp asked his friend Barry Tyler if he wanted to play football in the park.

I'D LIKE TO, RUBEN, BUT I'M WAITING FOR JESS. I'M TAKING HER TO THE MOVIES.

YOU NEVER WANT TO PLAY ANYMORE. YOU'VE BEEN GOING OUT WITH HER FOR WEEKS NOW.

▽ After the movie, Barry offered to buy Jess a hamburger.

THAT'S NICE OF YOU BARRY, BUT I HAVE TO BE GOING. I PROMISED MOM AND DAD I'D BE HOME BY 7:30. DON'T YOU HAVE TO GET BACK TOO?

I'M NOT IN ANY RUSH. IT'S LIKE A BATTLEFIELD AT HOME. MOM AND DAD ARE ALWAYS ARGUING. THEY WOULDN'T EVEN NOTICE IF I WASN'T THERE.

I'M SURE YOU'RE WRONG. MY PARENTS FIGHT A LOT TOO—AND THEY'RE NOT EVEN MARRIED! SERIOUSLY—IT'S JUST THEIR WAY. I KNOW THEY STILL LOVE EACH OTHER.

▷ Barry took Jess home and walked the short distance to his house.

I WISH I COULD BE SO SURE.

▽ The whole family was waiting for him. His older sister, Jodie, had brought her boyfriend, Raj, home.

BARRY, YOU'RE JUST IN TIME TO HEAR THE GOOD NEWS. RAJ AND I HAVE DECIDED TO MOVE IN TOGETHER.

▽ Barry told his grandma about Jess's parents not being married.

HONEST, GRANDMA, THEY'VE BEEN TOGETHER FOR NEARLY FIFTEEN YEARS.

WELL, I DON'T LIKE IT, I'M AFRAID. JODIE, YOU'RE AWFULLY YOUNG TO BE MAKING THIS KIND OF DECISION. YOU'VE OBVIOUSLY NOT THOUGHT IT THROUGH.

BUT YOU'RE NOT MARRIED!

THINGS ARE DIFFERENT THESE DAYS, MOM. I'M SURE THEY'LL GET MARRIED WHEN THEY'RE READY.

I THOUGHT YOU'D BE PLEASED FOR US. YOU NEVER THINK ABOUT ANYONE BUT YOURSELVES, DO YOU? JUST BECAUSE YOU TWO ARE SPLITTING UP DOESN'T MEAN RAJ AND I CAN'T BE HAPPY!

WHAT? IS IT TRUE?

OH, LEAVE THEM ALONE! I MIGHT HAVE KNOWN YOU'D MAKE A SCENE. YOU'RE SO POMPOUS.

PLEASE DON'T FIGHT!

IT CAN'T BE. I WON'T LET IT BE TRUE!

△ Barry's younger sister, Kate, ran out of the room, crying. Everyone was suddenly silent.

Barry is worried because his parents argue all the time.
Arguments can occur in even the best relationships. For some people, arguments are a way of expressing how they feel about a situation. Seeing and hearing your parents arguing can be very upsetting. They might not always realize the effect their arguments can have on you. However, this does not necessarily mean that they love each other or you any less.

Marriage is a public and formal expression of the way two people feel about each other.
In some cultures, marriages are arranged by parents for their children. Sometimes, the husband and wife might meet for the first time only shortly before the wedding is due to take place. Despite this, many arranged marriages are very successful.

Today, many couples choose not to marry, even though they may live together. Some people have strong views about this, believing that a couple should be married, especially if they have children. Others disagree. Whether or not two people are married need not affect their commitment to, and love for, each other and their children.

Relationships do not always stay the same.
Accepting that relationships change can be hard, because it means acknowledging that you will not always be as close to some people as you once were. For instance, the arrival of a new baby may mean some changes for everyone in the family. Or, it may be that, as you grow to know a person better, your feelings for that person change.

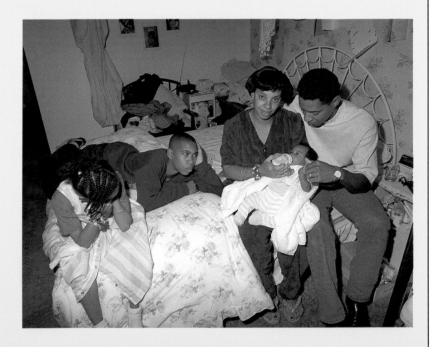

DIVORCE AND SEPARATION

A COUPLE WHO ARE NO LONGER HAPPY IN THEIR RELATIONSHIP MAY DECIDE TO SEPARATE. IF THEY ARE MARRIED, THEY MAY ALSO DECIDE TO DIVORCE.

Divorce is the legal end of a marriage. Until a divorce is confirmed, a couple remain married in the eyes of the law, whether or not they live together. A separation may also involve some legal issues. Some people see divorce as a more significant step than separation, because it brings an official end to a relationship. But whether or not two people are married, the process of separation and divorce is rarely easy for anyone concerned. For young people, the breakdown of their parents' relationship may raise strong emotions. It can often seem as though their feelings are not being considered. When an intimate relationship between two adults ends, they will no longer have a say in each other's life. A child might only live with one parent on a regular basis, but both parents may continue to share the responsibility of caring.

When a parent decides to live apart from his or her partner and children, it raises difficult feelings for everyone involved, including the adults who have made the decision to separate.

7

▷ Half an hour later, Barry was sitting on the sofa, talking to his mother. Jodie and Raj had left.

WHY DIDN'T YOU TELL ME BEFORE? YOU'VE OBVIOUSLY TOLD JODIE.

WE SHOULD HAVE, BARRY. I'M SORRY. WE DIDN'T WANT TO HURT YOU OR KATE.

WELL YOU HAVE, HAVEN'T YOU? BUT WHEN HAVE YOU EVER WORRIED ABOUT HOW WE FEEL?

THAT'S NOT FAIR, BARRY. YOU KNOW YOUR DAD AND I BOTH LOVE YOU. THIS ISN'T GOING TO BE THE END OF THE WORLD. THINGS WILL STILL BE THE SAME.

▽ Mr. Tyler came into the room. He had been upstairs talking to Kate.

DON'T SAY THAT, DEAR. IT ISN'T TRUE. AND IT WON'T MAKE IT ANY EASIER FOR BARRY OR KATE.

SHE'S CALMER NOW, BUT SHE'S STILL CRYING. I'VE PUT HER TO BED, BUT SHE WON'T FALL ASLEEP FOR A WHILE.

▽ Barry said he felt tired, and didn't want to talk about it anymore that night. He went up to Kate's room.

ARE YOU GOING TO GET A DIVORCE?

PERHAPS. WE'RE GOING TO SEPARATE FOR A WHILE FIRST.

WHY IS THIS HAPPENING, BARRY? I DON'T UNDERSTAND. I DON'T LIKE MOM AND DAD FIGHTING, BUT I WANT THEM BOTH TO BE HERE.

▽ Barry didn't sleep well that night. The next day, Ruben noticed something was wrong.

WHAT HAPPENED? DID YOU AND THE LOVELY JESS SPLIT UP?

I KNOW, KATE. SO DO I. THIS IS AWFUL. EVERYTHING'S GOING TO CHANGE.

NOT NOW, RUBEN. I'M NOT IN THE MOOD FOR JOKES.

▽ Ruben realized something was seriously the matter. Eventually, Barry decided to tell Ruben the truth.

▽ Barry hadn't realized that Ruben's dad was actually his stepfather.

I'M SORRY, BARRY. THE SAME THING HAPPENED TO ME, BUT I WAS A LOT YOUNGER. I DON'T REALLY REMEMBER MUCH ABOUT IT, BUT I KNOW THAT THE ATMOSPHERE AT HOME WAS TERRIBLE. THINGS GOT BETTER AFTER THEY SPLIT.

BUT HOW CAN THINGS BE BETTER? THEY WON'T BE TOGETHER.

MAYBE THEY WON'T GET DIVORCED. MOM SAID THEY'RE ONLY SEPARATING FOR NOW.

YOU'RE ALWAYS GOING ON ABOUT HOW MUCH THEY ARGUE. MY PARENTS WERE ALWAYS ARGUING. THEY DON'T ANYMORE. THEY'RE FRIENDS, IN FACT. DAD EVEN GETS ALONG WELL WITH MY STEPDAD.

▽ At home that evening, Kate talked to her grandma.

YOU DON'T UNDERSTAND. MOST OF THEM KEEP GOING ON ABOUT HOW GREAT THEIR PARENTS ARE.

SCHOOL WAS HORRIBLE TODAY, GRANDMA. I FELT LIKE EVERYONE WAS STARING AT ME. I DIDN'T TELL ANYONE ABOUT MOM AND DAD-NOT EVEN MY FRIENDS.

I DON'T THINK THEY'D BE AS SHOCKED AS YOU IMAGINE.

Finding out that your parents are going to separate can cause great distress.
This can be even worse if you are not told the truth about what is happening, or hear about it by accident, as Barry and Kate have done. Parents may be unsure how to tell their children about their decision. They may give different versions of the situation which make it more difficult to understand.

Many people who have divorced or separated remain friends, despite not wanting to be a couple anymore.
If two people have realized that they no longer love each other as close partners, or that their being together is only causing them and those around them distress, they may decide that breaking up is the most sensible solution.

   If the breakup itself is without a great deal of conflict, it can be easier for people to adjust to the new situation afterward. However, it is likely that any separation will create some difficult and unhappy feelings for everyone involved.

Some couples have a "trial separation."
They separate for a given length of time to sort out how they feel about each other. They may decide that they want to try again, or they may realize that they do need to be apart and decide to separate permanently. Trial separations can help adults to discover what they want and need, but the uncertainty during this time can be very confusing for young people.

WHY DO RELATIONSHIPS BREAK DOWN?

RELATIONSHIPS END FOR MANY REASONS. THE CAUSES MAY BE SIMILAR BUT EACH SITUATION WILL BE DIFFERENT.

The decision to separate or divorce may be made because of one specific action or might be the result of a build-up of circumstances. Some couples grow apart naturally, as their interests change. They may discover they no longer have very much in common. Not everyone has the same expectations of a relationship, and this might not become apparent until people have been living together for a while. Sometimes people go into a relationship believing they will be able to change aspects of the other person's behavior or attitude which they don't like. Physical or emotional abuse may be a factor in some breakups. Others seek sexual relationships with different people. This can make their partner feel jealous or betrayed. It is important to remember that the situations described above do not necessarily mean that a couple will decide to separate. Relationships which work well are the ones in which you can talk openly, and discuss any problems and concerns you have.

Just as best friends have arguments, so too do adults in a close relation- ship. Often the problems can be sorted out but some- times the nature of the relationship needs to change.

▽ The following weekend, Mr. Tyler moved out of the house.

▽ A couple of weeks later, Jodie and Raj came over. Mrs. Tyler had not yet arrived home from work.

▽ Things were still no better between Mr. and Mrs. Tyler.

▷ The next day, Barry talked to his mom alone.

▽ Neither of them saw Kate come into the kitchen.

HAVE YOU OR DAD MET SOMEONE ELSE? IS THAT WHY YOU'RE SEPARATING?

NO, DARLING, IT'S NOTHING LIKE THAT, I PROMISE.

PEOPLE DO SEPARATE BECAUSE THEY MEET SOMEONE ELSE, IT'S TRUE. BUT THAT'S NOT WHAT HAPPENED WITH YOUR FATHER AND ME. MAYBE YOUR GRANDMA'S RIGHT. SHE ALWAYS THOUGHT WE WERE MARRIED TOO YOUNG. WE DIDN'T WANT OUR MARRIAGE TO FAIL, BUT SOMETIMES THESE THINGS JUST HAPPEN.

▽ That evening, Barry found Kate crying in the yard. He asked her what was wrong.

IT'S ALL MY FAULT. I'M THE REASON DAD'S LEFT.

DON'T BE SILLY! WHY WOULD YOU THINK THAT?

I TOOK SOME MONEY FROM DAD'S COAT POCKET LAST WEEK, WITHOUT TELLING HIM. I'M BEING PAID BACK FOR DOING WRONG, LIKE GRANDMA ALWAYS SAYS.

I HEARD YOU TALKING TO MOM. SHE SAID THEY DIDN'T WANT TO BREAK UP. IT MUST BE BECAUSE OF SOMETHING I'VE DONE.

I'M SURE IT'S NOT LIKE THAT.

▽ A few days later, Barry and Jess went to the movies. He told her what Kate had said.

I KNOW KATE'S STORY COULDN'T BE TRUE, BUT SOMETIMES I WONDER IF IT ISN'T PARTLY OUR FAULT. I REMEMBER ALL THE TIMES MOM AND DAD WOULD ARGUE ABOUT US. MAYBE IF WE'D ACTED DIFFERENTLY IN SOME WAY THINGS WOULD BE OK.

BARRY, YOU'RE NOT TO BLAME FOR WHAT YOUR PARENTS DO. I'M SURE THEY'D TELL YOU THE SAME THING. COME ON, FORGET ABOUT IT FOR A WHILE. LET'S ENJOY THE MOVIE.

Kate has convinced herself that her parents' separation is in some way her fault.

If young people cannot understand the reason for their parents' decision to divorce or separate, they may wrongly assume that they are to blame. Or they may blame their brother or sister.

However, it is important to remember that although it is the adults' relationship which has broken down, they continue to be parents. Young people are not responsible for the behavior of, or the relationship between, their mom and dad.

The reasons for breakups are unlikely to be as simple as other people think.

When a couple separates, others close to them may have their own views about the decision. But it is often only the people who are closely involved who are fully aware of the circumstances. If a relationship is based on false hopes or understandings, it is less likely to survive than one which is based on trust and open communication.

Grandma believes today it is too easy to divorce.

It used to be much more difficult to obtain a divorce; it was only allowed under very special circumstances. Some people, like Grandma, think that couples will be tempted to divorce instead of working at a relationship. This may be true in some cases, but for many divorce is only a last resort. Lots of marriages and close relationships face problems, but are able to overcome them.

TAKING SIDES

IT IS NATURAL FOR YOUNG PEOPLE TO HAVE MIXED LOYALTIES WHEN THEIR PARENTS SEPARATE.

Children can come under a lot of pressure to take sides and support one parent against another. This is particularly true if people who are breaking up feel very hostile toward one another.

Some children may have a "favorite" parent. Or they might prefer being with mom for one activity and with dad for another. Suddenly feeling you have to choose one over another can be confusing and hurtful. It can create further tension if brothers and sisters disagree about which parent they feel their loyalty lies with. Adults sometimes forget that children have the right to be supportive of both parents, without feeling that they are being disloyal. This is especially true when other members of the family are already voicing their opinions and laying blame. Everyone might appear to have a different point of view. It can seem impossible to decide what the truth is, and who to believe. It helps to remember that each person involved will have his or her own understanding of the situation. You also have the right to form your opinions and should not feel disloyal about doing so.

Young people may sometimes feel torn between their parents. But it can also be painful for a parent to come to terms with the fact that his or her child will continue to love and support the other parent.

▽ It was a few months later. One day, Kate came home just as her mom was slamming the telephone receiver down.

I DON'T KNOW WHAT I EVER SAW IN YOUR DAD. I'M REALLY GLAD NONE OF YOU TAKE AFTER HIM.

WHY DO YOU HAVE TO TALK ABOUT DAD LIKE THAT? YOU'RE HORRIBLE.

▽ Kate ran up to her room. Later, her mom tried to talk to her.

I WISH I COULD LIVE WITH DAD.

I KNOW IT'S HARD FOR YOU AND BARRY. IT'S HARD FOR ME, TOO. I'M SORRY ABOUT WHAT I SAID. I NEED YOU HERE, KATE.

▽ The following weekend was Barry's birthday. His mom arranged a small party for him.

THANKS, MOM. IT'S GREAT. JUST WHAT I WANTED.

NO IT'S NOT. YOU SAID YOU WANTED YOUR TEAM'S NEW FOOTBALL JERSEY.

I KNOW. I'M SORRY, BARRY. I JUST COULDN'T AFFORD IT. I'LL GET YOU IT SOON, I PROMISE.

▽ His mom walked away. Barry turned to Kate.

WHY DID YOU SAY THAT? WHY ARE YOU SO AGAINST MOM THESE DAYS?

SHE'S SO MEAN TO DAD. I DON'T THINK SHE CARES WHAT WE THINK. I REALLY MISS HIM.

▽ Mr. Tyler arrived a little while later with Barry's present. He'd bought him the football jersey.

THANKS, DAD.

SEE, DAD CARES. HAVE YOU BOUGHT ME SOMETHING, DAD?

WELL, IT'S NOT YOUR BIRTHDAY, PRINCESS. STILL, I THINK I MIGHT HAVE A PRESENT FOR YOU, TOO.

▽ After his dad left, Barry danced with Jess. He said his mom was upset.

SHE SAID DAD'S JUST TRYING TO BUY OUR LOYALTY. I DON'T KNOW WHAT TO BELIEVE ANYMORE.

During the separation, you may hear different versions of what is going on.
Trying to make sense of a situation when you are being given conflicting information is never easy. Hearing other people saying nasty things about someone you love is also upsetting. It is important to remember that you have the right to your own views. Your feelings about your mom or dad do not have to change just because their feelings for each other have.

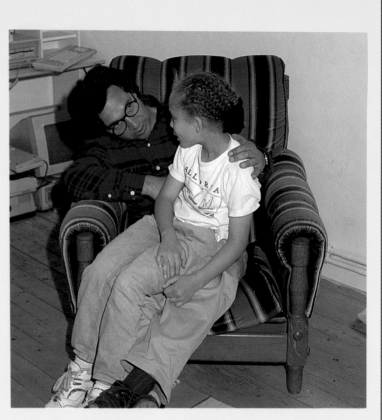

Mr. Tyler has bought presents for Barry and Kate.
A divorced or separated parent might feel the need to treat his or her children. This can be because he or she wants to show the children how much they are loved or to make up for any unhappiness that the breakup has caused.

Sometimes this is a way of the parent trying to establish a new role within the family. It can make you feel special, but it can also be difficult for the other parent, particularly if he or she is not in a position to do the same.

Sometimes adults take out their feelings about each other on the children.
After a divorce or separation, adults often feel unsure of themselves and their position with their children. They may ask their children which parent they love most. They are probably doing this because of their own confusion, but it only makes the situation harder for young people. You may think that whatever you say or do will be wrong, because you will be betraying one parent by agreeing with the other. It is best to be honest about how you feel.

ATTITUDES TOWARD DIVORCE

ALTHOUGH DIVORCE AND SEPARATION ARE MORE ACCEPTED TODAY, THERE ARE THOSE WHO STILL HOLD STRONG VIEWS ABOUT THE SUBJECT.

For many people, marriage is for life, and divorce is not an option. This may be because of their religious or cultural beliefs.
Some people believe that couples should stay together, no matter what difficulties arise. Others disagree. They see no reason, for instance, why a person who is being mistreated within a marriage or other close relationship should have to put up with it. Another view is that divorce should be allowed, provided there are no children involved. On the other hand, young people who are miserable because their parents are always arguing or obviously no longer love each other, may feel a sense of relief when the decision to separate is made. The reality is that there are no easy answers. In each case it is up to the people within the relationship to try to decide what is best for them.

Some religions and cultures take the view that divorce is never acceptable. Some marriage services stress that, no matter what, the couple's commitment is to each other, and is for life.

▽ The following month saw the start of the school vacation. Jess invited some friends to her house one afternoon.

△ Everyone started to talk about marriage and relationships.

▽ The next day, Mr. Tyler came to the house. He and Mrs. Tyler had some news.

△ Mr. and Mrs. Tyler talked to Barry and Kate for a while. Everyone was very upset.

Some young people are ashamed to admit that their parents are separating.
But as Barry has discovered, lots of his friends have been through the same thing. It is normal to experience all kinds of different emotions during your parents' divorce. Talking with good friends about some aspects of the situation, and listening to their opinion, may help you to understand more about it.

Kate is certain that her mom and dad will get back together again.
Some young people hold on to the belief that their parents will eventually decide that they do want to live with each other, despite the divorce or even after one or both parents have remarried. However hard and upsetting it is, refusing to admit what you know to be the truth will not help you to deal with the situation. It can make the feelings you have even more difficult to cope with.

Some people believe that a couple should stay together if they have children, whatever the difficulties in their relationship.
The upheaval of their parents' divorce or separation can be very hard on young people. But in some cases, living with parents who are very unhappy with each other may present just as many problems. Remember that each situation is unique. Most couples will have considered carefully the effect their decision might have on their children.

THE DIVORCE PROCESS

ANY COUPLE IS ABLE TO SEPARATE WITHOUT TAKING LEGAL ACTION. A DIVORCE, HOWEVER, IS A LEGAL PROCESS.

The rules for granting a divorce vary from country to country. In most cases, though, the decision will depend on certain factors.
There are many reasons why people apply for a divorce and why a divorce is granted. It may be on the grounds of mental cruelty, or actual physical abuse from their partner. Or it might be that a person has had a sexual relationship outside the marriage. Divorce is usually allowed if two people have lived apart for a certain period of time. In many situations, both partners have agreed that divorce is the best choice. Sometimes, however, they may have serious disagreements about various points. These are often to do with financial matters and each person's role in bringing up children from the relationship. In these cases it can take a long time for people to sort out the details, and in the end the courts may have to decide. The law can also require one adult to give up a portion of his or her earnings, in order to support the other partner or any children involved.

In some countries, couples are required by law to undergo counselling. This is to make sure they have thought carefully about the situation and are sure that they have found the best solution.

▽ One afternoon soon afterward, Jodie and Raj came over. Mr. and Mrs. Tyler had gone to see their lawyer.

WHY DO THEY NEED A LAWYER?

DIVORCE IS A LEGAL PROCESS. THEY NEED SOMEONE WHO CAN HELP THEM WITH ALL THE DETAILS.

SUCH AS WHAT?

BECAUSE MOM AND DAD OWN THE HOUSE AND EVERYTHING TOGETHER, BUT AREN'T GOING TO BE MARRIED ANYMORE, THEY HAVE TO DECIDE HOW TO DIVIDE THE PROPERTY.

▷ They explained about the decisions that would have to be made.

THEY ALSO HAVE TO MAKE ARRANGEMENTS TO MAKE SURE YOUR DAD GIVES YOUR MOM ENOUGH MONEY TO LOOK AFTER YOU.

DAD TOLD US IT'S EASIER IF WE GO ON LIVING HERE WITH MOM. EVEN THEN THEY DIDN'T REALLY ASK HOW WE FELT ABOUT IT.

SOMETIMES IT FEELS AS THOUGH WE'RE BEING LEFT OUT OF EVERYTHING. ALL THESE DECISIONS ARE BEING MADE ABOUT WHAT'S GOING TO HAPPEN AND WE FIND OUT AFTERWARD. IT'S NOT FAIR.

I KNOW, BUT THINGS ARE SOMETIMES MUCH WORSE THAN THIS. I REMEMBER MY BEST FRIEND'S PARENTS DIVORCED WHEN SHE WAS YOUR AGE. IT WAS TERRIBLE. THEY FOUGHT OVER EVERYTHING. THEY HAD TO SELL THE HOUSE. THEY COULDN'T AGREE ABOUT WHO THE CHILDREN SHOULD LIVE WITH. IN THE END, THE COURTS HAD TO DECIDE.

I JUST WISH MOM AND DAD WOULD TALK TO US MORE — EXPLAIN WHAT'S GOING ON.

I KNOW IT'S HARD. IT'S HARD FOR ME TOO.

◁ Barry said it was different for Jodie, because she didn't live there anymore.

△ Jodie said that divorces can go on for a long time.

DON'T FORGET THEY'RE GOING THROUGH A LOT TOO, KATE. THERE'S A LOT TO SORT OUT.

SOMETIMES PEOPLE GET SO CAUGHT UP IN EVERYTHING THAT THEY FORGET ABOUT OTHER THINGS — THINGS THAT MATTER JUST AS MUCH. YOU JUST HAVE TO BE PATIENT.

I KNOW. IT JUST TAKES A LOT OF GETTING USED TO.

When a couple are married or live together, most of the things they own often belong to both of them. If they divorce, they will need to make arrangements, as Barry and Kate's mom and dad are doing, to transfer ownership of their belongings to each partner separately. This can be done without conflict but sometimes there are disagreements about who gets what. Parents might become so caught up with this, that they forget how upsetting this can be for the children.

After a divorce, children will usually live for most of the time with just one parent.
Which parent this should be is often the decision of the family itself. If parents are unable to agree, the courts may be asked to decide. The well-being of the children will be the most important factor in this. Even so, the final decision might not agree with your own understanding of what you feel is best. It is not always easy to accept the situation, particularly if people don't appear to be taking your feelings into consideration.

Most couples, like Mr. and Mrs. Tyler, will seek the advice of a lawyer at some point.
This is particularly true when the terms of a divorce are contested by one of the partners. Then the courts may become involved. Lawyers, mediators, and counselors can help people to come to terms with their decision, and to understand what it will mean for them and their family in the future.

THE EFFECTS OF DIVORCE AND SEPARATION

A SEPARATION OR DIVORCE WILL USUALLY INVOLVE SOME EMOTIONAL UPHEAVAL FOR EVERYONE CONCERNED.

It takes time to come to terms with the fact that your parents will no longer be together.

Although young people's reactions may differ according to their age, most will experience a range of feelings. Some young people become angry. They want to blame someone for what has happened. Or they refuse to accept the situation, hoping that things will return to how they used to be. Sometimes they might feel guilty, believing that they could have done something to alter the situation. A young person may feel helpless, thinking that he or she has no control at all over what is going on.

People's sense of self-worth can be affected by the changes at home. This might also influence their behavior. For instance, some children refuse to go to school, or throw tantrums. Younger children may become anxious or want a lot of attention. Older children may become withdrawn or aggressive. All of these are natural reactions to a difficult and confusing situation.

It can make young people feel very lonely if they feel that differently-aged brothers or sisters don't really understand what is going on.

▽ A few weeks later, Jodie and Raj had some news of their own.

IT'S A SHAME DAD ISN'T HERE, BUT WE THOUGHT YOU'D WANT TO KNOW. WE'VE DECIDED TO GET MARRIED.

DARLING THAT'S WONDERFUL NEWS. I'M SO PLEASED FOR YOU BOTH.

▽ The following evening, Jess and Barry went out again. He told her about Jodie and Raj.

I CAN'T BELIEVE IT. I THINK YOUR PARENTS HAVE THE RIGHT IDEA. IT'S BEST NOT TO MARRY, THEN YOU DON'T HAVE ALL THE HASSLE IF THINGS GO WRONG.

THAT'S NOT TRUE. IT WOULD BE JUST AS DIFFICULT FOR ME IF MY PARENTS DECIDED TO SEPARATE.

IF THEY EVER DID, THAT DOESN'T MEAN I'D NEVER GET MARRIED OR LIVE WITH SOMEONE.

▷ Jess said that was silly. He might feel like that now, but he'd change his mind when he was older.

HOW DO YOU KNOW? I'M BEGINNING TO WONDER IF IT'S ALL WORTH IT.

YOU'RE NOT CONCENTRATING KATE, IS SOMETHING THE MATTER?

▽ At school, the teacher had noticed that Kate was not her usual self in class.

I DON'T WANT TO DO THIS. WORK'S STUPID!

▽ Kate threw her book down and ran out of the classroom. That evening the teacher called Mrs. Tyler in.

KATE'S A GOOD STUDENT. SHE WAS DOING REALLY WELL, BUT LATELY SHE'S CHANGED. SHE'S BECOME MOODY. SOMETIMES SHE CAN BE VERY DIFFICULT TO HANDLE DURING LESSONS.

▽ At home, Kate and her mom talked.

I KNOW YOU AND DAD DON'T LOVE EACH OTHER ANYMORE, BUT I STILL LOVE YOU BOTH. I FEEL LIKE I'VE GOT TO CHOOSE BETWEEN YOU.

AS YOU KNOW, MY HUSBAND AND I ARE DIVORCING. I THINK IT'S HIT KATE REALLY HARD. I'LL TALK TO HER.

OH, KATE. YOU DON'T HAVE TO LOVE ONE OF US MORE THAN THE OTHER. WHATEVER YOUR DAD AND I FEEL ABOUT EACH OTHER, WE BOTH STILL LOVE YOU VERY MUCH.

Parents' divorce or separation might mean losing touch with those you care about.
Young people may have to move to live with one of their parents. This might mean that they are no longer able to see their friends. Some adults try to prevent their children from seeing their absent parent or members of his or her family. It can feel unfair and hurtful if one parent chooses not to see the children. It is also very hard, for both parents and child, if a child decides not to have any contact with the absent parent.

Bottling up your feelings does not make them go away.
The emotions that young people have when parents separate or divorce may take some time to deal with. Although it might be hard to know who to speak to, especially if you think you can no longer talk to your parents, it can help to express your feelings.

Barry's parents' divorce has made him question the value of marriage.
It is natural to have these kinds of feelings but remember that every relationship is different. Jess knows that only she and a future partner can decide what is right for them. Letting this sort of situation influence your outlook only puts barriers in the way of potentially strong relationships.

NEW BEGINNINGS

YOUNG PEOPLE OFTEN HAVE VERY LITTLE SAY IN THEIR PARENTS' DECISION TO SEPARATE OR DIVORCE. TO THEM IT CAN SEEM LIKE THE END OF EVERYTHING.

In a way, in fact, it is the start of a new period in their life. However, recognizing this will mean understanding that some changes are inevitable. This is often very difficult.

You may be told that a divorce is final. This does not always mean that you have reached the stage where you are ready to accept it. The emotions people have during the breakup of a relationship have been compared to those of people who are grieving for someone who has died. It can take a long time to come to terms fully with the situation. It is important to consider how parents may be feeling as well. They have been used to being part of a couple. Adjusting to being in social situations on their own may be difficult. Many adults begin new relationships. This might mean young people becoming part of a new family situation, and perhaps getting used to the idea of having stepbrothers or sisters. Seeing one parent only at set times may seem unfair. Some young people have felt guilty because, although they have wanted to see their mom or dad, the time for visits clashes with time they would otherwise have spent with friends. If this happens, talking honestly about how you feel can help to solve the problem.

It is not always easy to accept that your parents will eventually carry on with their lives and may meet new partners.

▽ It was some months later, Mr. and Mrs. Tyler's divorce was now final. For the first time in a long while, they were all together at Jodie and Raj's wedding.

▽ After the ceremony, Mr. Tyler spoke to Barry and Kate.

▽ At the party afterward, Barry noticed his mom looking rather sad. He asked if she was OK.

▽ Barry went to join his friends.

WHO'S THAT?

THAT'S SHEILA, DAD'S NEW FRIEND. THEY'VE BEEN GOING OUT FOR A WHILE. WE'VE ONLY MET HER A COUPLE OF TIMES, THOUGH.

SHE'S OK, BUT SHE'S TRYING TOO HARD TO BE NICE. SHE WANTS US TO LIKE HER.

WILL SHEILA BE COMING WITH US?

SHE COULD IF YOU'D LIKE HER TO. OR WE CAN BE ON OUR OWN.

BRING HER ALONG IF YOU LIKE. SHE MIGHT KEEP YOU FROM BEING LATE!

DON'T FORGET—I'LL PICK YOU UP NEXT SATURDAY AT 10:00. THINK ABOUT WHAT YOU WOULD LIKE TO DO OVER THE WEEKEND.

I'M FINE, DARLING, HONEST. IT'S JUST A BIG DAY. IT'S STRANGE TO HAVE YOUR DAD HERE, THAT'S ALL.

WAS MOM OK? I SAW YOU TALKING TO HER.

YES. I THINK SHE'S A BIT UPSET ABOUT DAD AND SHEILA, BUT SHE'S ALL RIGHT.

YOU BOTH SEEM TO BE GETTING ALONG BETTER.

THAT'S TRUE. I TOLD YOU EVERYTHING WOULD WORK OUT.

IT'S STILL ODD, NOT HAVING DAD AROUND. I REALLY MISS HIM SOMETIMES.

YOU TWO BOTH SEEM HAPPIER ABOUT THE SITUATION NOW.

I KNOW. BUT HE AND MOM BOTH SEEM HAPPIER APART. WE'LL GET USED TO IT ALL, AND THINGS WILL GO ON FROM THERE.

Like Mr. Tyler, many divorced or separated people begin new relationships.
Some decide to remarry. Accepting a new person in your mom or dad's life can be very hard. You may feel betrayed. You may think he or she is trying to replace your other parent. Even if one or both of your parents does not seem any happier after the breakup, this does not mean that you should not feel able to enjoy yourself. It takes time for everyone.

Barry and Kate only see their dad on weekends now.
It is important to remember that just because you only see your mom or dad occasionally, it doesn't mean you can't talk to each other at different times. Nor does it mean that he or she loves you any less.

When parents separate or divorce, you may feel as though your life will never be the same again.
The breakup of any relationship can leave people feeling hurt and confused. It may not be easy, but people do adjust to new situations.

Although things are not the same as before, with time you may come to realize that the change can have a positive side. Parents' separation or divorce means the end of one period of your life. It is also the beginning of another, for everyone involved.

Special occasions, such as birthdays or school events, where two parents may often be involved, can present you with difficult and conflicting emotions. Feeling guilty about circumstances which are not your responsibility does not help. Try talking openly and honestly with your parents.

WHAT CAN WE DO?

HAVING READ THIS BOOK, YOU WILL UNDERSTAND MORE ABOUT SEPARATION AND DIVORCE, AND THE EFFECT THEY CAN HAVE ON EVERYONE CONCERNED.

The breakdown of a relationship can be difficult for everyone involved.
If you know someone whose parents are splitting up, or if your own parents are separating, understanding the kinds of emotions everyone might be going through can help. Feeling depressed, angry, or confused, looking for someone to blame – these are all common reactions. It is important to learn how to cope with and express these feelings. Most people do adjust and are able to get on with their lives by accepting the new situation and taking things from there.

Active Parenting
810 Franklin Court
Suite B
Marietta, GA 30067
(800) 825-0060

Children's Rights Council
220 I Street, N.E.
Suite 230
Washington, DC 20002
(800) 787-KIDS

Family Service America
11700 W. Lake Park Drive
Milwaukee, WI 53224
(800) 221-2681

ADULTS CAN ALSO HELP, BY REALIZING THAT MOST CHILDREN WANT TO KNOW WHAT IS HAPPENING, AND BY BEING AS HONEST AS POSSIBLE ABOUT THEIR DECISION.

It is sometimes easy for adults who are divorcing or separating to forget that, just as they might be feeling upset themselves, their children may also be deeply affected.
Young people and adults who have read this book together might find it helpful to discuss how they feel about the issues raised, and to share their ideas and experiences. Anyone who would like to have more information, or to talk to someone not directly involved, may be able to obtain advice or support from the organizations listed below.

Kids' Rights
10100 Park Cedar Drive
Charlotte, NC 28210
(800) 892-5437

The Beginning Experience
305 Michigan Ave.
Detroit, MI 48226
(313) 965-5110

Parents Sharing Custody
420 S. Beverley Drive
Suite 100
Beverley Hills
CA 90212-4410
(310) 286-9171

Single Parent Resource Center
141 W. 28th Street
Suite 302
New York, NY 10001
(212) 947-0221

Divorce Support
5020 W. School Street
Chicago, IL 60641
(312) 286-4541

Rainbows
1111 Tower Road
Schaumburg, IL 60173
(847) 310-1880

Parent Without Partners
401 N. Michigan Ave.
Chicago, IL 60611-4267
(312) 644-6610

Children's Rights Projects
132 W. 43rd Street
6th Floor
New York, NY 10036
(212) 944-9800

Divorced Parents X-Change
P.O. Box 1127
Athens,
OH 45701-1127
(614) 664-2114

INDEX

Photocredits
All the pictures in this book are by Roger Vlitos apart from: page 18; Frank Spooner.
The publishers wish to acknowledge that all of the photographs in this book have been
posed by models.